What I Learned: Poems

poems by

Elizabeth S. Wolf

Finishing Line Press
Georgetown, Kentucky

What I Learned: Poems

Copyright © 2017 by Elizabeth S. Wolf
ISBN 978-1-63534-324-3 First Edition
All rights reserved under International and Pan-American Copyright Conventions.
No part of this book may be reproduced in any manner whatsoever without written permission from the publisher, except in the case of brief quotations embodied in critical articles and reviews.

ACKNOWLEDGMENTS

I am grateful to the editors for previously publishing some of the poems in this chapbook:
"to Norman" and "Night clouds." appeared in *National Poetry Journal* April 1986
"Borderlines" and "The Minister's Wife" appeared in *Merrimac Mic Anthology: Gleanings from the First Year* March 2015 and in *Mosaics: A Collection of Independent Women* Volume 1 March 2016
"Germanwings 9525"and "Grateful for Good Neighbors" appeared online in the *Scarlet Leaf Review* February 2016
"Every Addict is Somebody's Child", "What If" and "Because" appeared online in the *Scarlet Leaf Review* March 2016. "What If" also published in *The Best of Kindness: Origami Poems Project* April 2016
"Yes Sir" and "Visiting Frank at the V.A." appeared in *Peregrine* (Volume 30) May 2016
"Red Riding Redux" appeared in *Merrimac Mic Anthology III: The River Widens* March 2017

Publisher: Leah Maines

Editor: Christen Kincaid

Cover Art: Samantha Graves

Author Photo: Samantha Graves

Cover Design: Elizabeth Maines McCleavy

Printed in the USA on acid-free paper.
Order online: www.finishinglinepress.com
also available on amazon.com

Author inquiries and mail orders:
Finishing Line Press
P. O. Box 1626
Georgetown, Kentucky 40324
U. S. A.

Table of Contents

What I Learned as a Graduate Student of Cognitive Neuroscience 1

Borderlines 2

Yes Sir 3

The Minister's Wife 4

Red Riding Redux 5

Night clouds. 6

Revelation 7

Visiting Frank at the V.A. 8

to Norman 9

Character Study #1 10

for Ben 14

Germanwings 9525 16

Grateful for Good Neighbors 23

Off the Trail 24

Every Addict is Somebody's Child 25

Unarmed Combat: A Report from the Front 27

Because 31

What If 32

We are what we do, what we experience, what we learn. We humans build stories and theories about it all, and we live within those stories, those interpretations of all of these constantly impinging experiences. That is what we are and that is how it works. Full stop.
—Michael S. Gazzaniga, *Shifting Gears: Seeking New Approaches for Mind/ Brain Mechanisms* 2013

The belief that there is only one truth and that oneself is in possession of it, seems to me the deepest root of all that is evil in the world.
—Max Born, *Natural Philosophy of Cause and Chance* 1964

What I Learned as a Graduate Student of Cognitive Neuroscience

Close your eyes, child.
Tell me what you see.
                        I cannot see with my eyes closed.

Close your eyes, child.
Open your mind.
Tell me what you see.
                        I cannot see with my eyes closed.

Close your eyes, child.
Open your mind.
Open your heart.
Tell me what you see.
                        Ooooooooohh.

Tell me what you see, child.
                        Is it real?

Stories are the only reality there is.

Borderlines

Sometimes I walked all night and slept at school during the day, under a table, behind the blinds, beside the beds in the boarding boys' dorm. I wasn't at Kent State but I was wounded; I wasn't at the Watergate but eavesdropping devices were trying to steal my secrets while murmuring lies. I was not a crook. I was born the same year as that girl running down the road in Vietnam, naked, limbs akimbo, burning from the napalm, fleeing from the fire. Sometimes my skin sloughed off in sheets. Nights I was too tired to walk I hid between the prickly ornamental bushes and the stolid foundations of suburban homes. I sang Blowing in the Wind, I sang Long Black Veil, softly, over and over, waiting for the sun, for safe passage. I found snakes in the landscaping, waddling skunks, broken-necked bodies of birds that had crashed into clean clear windows. I sang Amazing Grace when I buried the birds. I forgot how to pray, I forgot how to cry, I forgot to be scared of tests given at school, I forgot nice ladies wore gloves into town, I forgot there was a better day coming. I kept on keeping on. I shut my eyes but still I saw; I hid screaming but made no sound. I survived.

I survived. I bend, I blend: I am your neighbor, I am your friend. I feed your kids cut fruit and chocolate milk; I rinse dishes in a double sink. I keep a tidy, orderly house. Screens shield the windows. Sometimes my mind spins and scenery sways but I hold my head high: nobody knows where I've been. At night I lock up tight. I am on the inside, in the warmth, in the dry; indeed, I survived.

Yes Sir

yes sir we said yes
sir whenever he was angry,
my father, he would start in with
"listen, my friend" and we knew whatever
he said next the answer was "yes, sir" and
maybe just maybe you could escape but
today he is inflamed, he is flushed, he is
quivering mad and we scramble to get out of
his way and he storms over to the closet and
finds an old flag, from where we don't know—
maybe his father's grave—and he
sticks it on a pole, rams it into the front yard,
grabs my brother's trumpet and tries
to play taps, to play reveille, the world
has gone reeling mad, the neighbors all know and
pretend not to see: he is marching us now
yes sir around the yard racing and
screaming yes sir the flag snapping at
the corners, the corners they fold down smooth
in a tight triangle and salute when they strip
the flag from his coffin to present to
my mother but she steps back, so
they pass it to me, but
I don't know what to do so
I stand straight and respond
yes, sir.

The Minister's Wife

She stared at me intently
through the slightly swollen eye
she swore that she had gotten by
falling down the stairs.
I never saw her take
a single clumsy step
but every time I left the house
she had a silly accident
and wore another bruise.
Listen to me, she insisted.
This is truly something
you can always count on.
There are three parts water
to one part concentrate
in each and every pitcher
of frozen orange juice.
That's the American way.

Red Riding Redux

The Big Bad Wolf has
gleaming eyes and sharp teeth
and he is crooning "Little Red,
Little Red" and even though
I probably shouldn't, I always
go to him. My bad.

The Big Bad Wolf is
full of want, and it is always
all about him. I may resent
doing the dishes and the washing
but then, that toothy grin…
I used to wear red but now
it's faded to mousy brown.
I'm fading too.

The Big Bad Wolf sleeps in.
This gives me time to pack.
I take my stuff and the stuff
my mother left me and
not much else. I don't need
souvenirs. I hit the road
mid-morning, leaving a sink full of
pots and pans, a closet full of
lingerie, my lingering shame.
Red Riding rises again.

Night clouds.

The sky is out tonight.
I clench my hands into fists
to fight the chill, and ward off
any attempt to count time
on my fingers.
I open my eyes fiercely
refusing to see
pages from a calendar
soaking up the rich red blood
of my imagination.
Seven months have passed
since my child wasn't born.
Stubbornly I cling
to the list of rationales
that supported me then
as now. And why not
believe?
Still I sometimes shiver
to see a candle
snuffed.
One flick of the wrist
and the flame
is over.

Revelation
> *"If I were to tell you what I see,*
> *would you love me still?"*
> —Janet Longe Sadler

Here in the pale green hallways
a skeleton is staring, drugged eyes
sunk in bony sockets; he tried to
starve himself, wasted away to
frailty and chills; now he munches
rye toast, walking slowly on skinny
white legs, leaving a trail of
dry crumbs; walks passed the jew who
decided one night that he was
the true jesus; who walked out
barefoot through the snow,
proclaiming his message and all
that was divine; who was carried back in
raving and now sits rocking, rocking,
rocking, cradling feet swathed in
white bandages, covering blackened
frostbitten skin, nearly lost
toes; he believes the doctors
down in the ER drained all of his
powers, all of his sacred love;
he seeks his debrided skin as if
the shredded scales are holy, as if
we could still be saved.

Visiting Frank at the V.A.

There's nothing special about Tuesday to make it Tuesday: no particular smell or taste or pattern to the lavender bloom in the clouds at sunrise. We all memorize a string of words and that's what we call every row of days. It's called mind control, lady, and it don't work on me.

I call today purple loosestrife because that's the first picture I had in my head when I opened my eyes. I didn't go to the right "activities" for a "Tuesday" but I sure as hell know what purple-loosestrife-day means. It looks like a pretty flower, but it's an invader… when carried someplace new, it beats up the native plants and takes over the swamp.

I've been here since the month of firm firry frosts. They call it October but I called it Jack, until paper cut-outs of turkeys went up on the wall. Then I called it Tom. Now there are hearts up by the bulletin board and I call it Lucille. I had a friend named Lucille once, a sweet girl. She raised pansies in her window box. Or maybe it was huskies. I think maybe I married her. The C.O. would know. You know, you kind of look like Lucy. Or maybe like her mother.

They say I'll be here a long time but that's o.k. This is where I woke up purple-loosestrife morning. I have no place to go, may as well bunk here. When might I go home? Is this another test? Give it up, lady. I ain't playing around. Hey, hey, no waterworks. That crap don't work on me.

to Norman

You came from an ancient reservation:
a painted mesa surrounded by
sacred spirits. As a child
you learned grandmother's stories,
watched dancers down from the mountains
etched into the night by the flickering fire
   shadows leap and writhe still
      in the black depths of your eyes—
Sometimes after the ceremonies
the police took your father away
drunk. Other times they didn't
and you lay listening to the rhythm
of the thumps and grunts as he
beat your mother. Now you sit
amidst the clamor and fire-engine wails
of downtown Phoenix. My mission
is to convince you that 2 pints
equals 1 quart
and drill for multiplication tables.

Character Study #1

The older daughter, Nora,
had dark hair, dark eyes,
an impish look, almond brown skin.
I say older but she was maybe 4,
not in school, always dancing or
jiggling or making up songs or
hanging on her mother, who was
always frustrated with her. Just go
do something! her mother would say.
Now! Somewhere else! Nora
always hovered, always
at the edge, never at rest.
The younger daughter

Bernie had fair hair, a
chubby toddler tummy,
and a hare lip. They had started
treatment for her palate but still
when she spoke, no one but her mother
or Nora understood. Her mother's boyfriend,
Ron, used to say: Bernie speaks Russian.
Ron had fair hair and the start of a
beer gut but they said Ron was
not the father. Both girls,
dark and fair,

were from Deb's first husband,
Carl. Carl was older and walked painfully
on two canes. I knew this because
we stayed overnight at his house,
while the girls visited. There was a
fountain in the courtyard and we slept in one room
with bunkbeds. I was in my early twenties,

my boyfriend worked with Deb's boyfriend,
we had no boundaries and odd events
happened all the time.

Deb told me it was a bad marriage.
Carl was cruel, abusive; when she had
Bernie she was afraid to leave
Nora in his care. For a few months
Nora had a foster family. And again,
during the divorce, or maybe
they were together in a shelter,
it was never clear. I don't remember
when Deb and her girls met Ron.
It was before I drove west, ending up
with my boyfriend in Arizona (odd events
happen all the time). Mostly Deb told me

Ron was a nice guy, the best. He didn't
let her have a car—where did she
need to go, with two little kids?
But they rarely fought. Deb was
happy to be at home. Life wasn't
always this good, she told me,
one afternoon, after I had driven her
to run errands. We sat drinking beer
while the girls played in a shallow
Walmart wading pool. Deb told me
about being fourteen and fighting with
her own mom, constantly,
fiercely. Deb's mom grew up
on the reservation and threatened
to send Deb back home, to learn
the old ways. Deb ran away with a friend,

then met a guy, the friend went home,
and Deb ended up

turning tricks, somehow in Hawaii. One day
she was sitting on a dirty bedspread,
staring, stoned, not caring anymore,
and a guy came into her room. She assumed
it was her next John but it was her step dad,
come to take her home. She didn't look at faces
then. Odd things happen all the time.

Ron's such a nice guy, Deb told me. But still.
Sometimes they fought, the kids got on his nerves,
especially Nora, always *always* in the way.
So Deb had a plan. She put saccharine tablets
in her monthly pill packets.
She flushed the pills. She figured
she'd be pregnant soon. And then
Ron couldn't leave—then
he would stay forever.

I drank a little more. Even in my early twenties
I knew this was a bad plan. I played horseshoes
with Nora. I asked if she was excited
to start school. Yes! she said,
looking at her mom. Later Nora asked
if I knew where school was, and if she would
have to go away. I told her I'd find her school
and maybe we could drive over
with mom and Bernie and visit.
Nora liked that plan. I don't remember
if we ever did it.

I moved home to New England,
without the boyfriend. I grew up.
I don't know what happened to that
family. I carried a picture of the four of them
in my wallet for years, a family portrait
from Sears. Deb and Ron were smiling straight
into the camera. Bernie was looking down
at a stuffed dog in her lap. Nora, for once
not in motion, was looking up at her
mother, making sure she was still there
after the flash was gone.

for Ben

There's a tear in the world:
Ben has flown free. He put down
a bottle; he picked up
a gun. In that flash
it was finished. There are no
take-backs. There is no
next level. For Ben,
there is no more pain.
There's a Ben-shaped
tear in the world:
We are all left behind.

And we sob. We can't believe
and then we can't think of
anything else. We can't eat
              we eat junk.
We can't sleep
              we nap through class.
We cling to each other
              we all die alone.
We forget why we walked
into a room. We vow to never forget
sweet, awkward Ben.
There's a tear in the world:
Ben has flown free.
We are all left behind.

Trauma teachers tell us
it will get better, with time.
              Ben is outside of time
We will find a new normal.
          we will never
         feel normal
        again.

We mingle in the churchyard
surrounded by sturdy orange pumpkins.
           I want to smash the smug pumpkins.
We tell stories, of the bright boy who knew
all of the presidents, vice-presidents, and major achievements
of each administration
           dude could kill a bottle of vodka in two days.
of the good friend who always listened and
brought bags of candy.
           dude did you see the slices all up his arms?
Did the police talk to you? Was he bullied?
           dude remember when he made a Facebook page
           as Eric Harris?
He was so talented, on the computer, with his videos.
           dude did you know he made Columbine mashups?
           dubbed over the old security footage with
           soundtrack and screams, it was raw—
           dude it was totally sick—

Why didn't anyone see any signs? Wasn't there anything
we could have done?

We file into pews, to pray, to sing hymns, surrounded by
pictures of Ben with family and friends, with his
date to the homecoming dance
(my daughter). When six 15 year old boys
rise as young men to carry the coffin
through tears I see how their faces will be set
years from now, when their parents pass,

or their wives leave, or
(God forbid) they bury a child.
All the losses of their lives
will now be measured
in magnitudes of Ben.

Germanwings 9525
24 March 2015

It was a mild mid-morning in March
when the plane, after a short delay, took off
from Barcelona. There were 56 empty
seats; there were 144 passengers
on board; there were 6 crew members.
There were no survivors.

There were 16 German high school students
heading home that Tuesday. Sixteen lives on the cusp,
aborted. The girl in row 16 sobbed,
wished she had kissed that boy who stared at her,
wished she had hugged her mother and not
turned away, not refused to let her mother help
pack and carry her bag. *Iche liebe meine
mutter*, she says, over and over, her stomach in her
ears, her ears throbbing, now she is screaming,
I love my mother.

The pilot knocks at the
locked cockpit door.
The copilot breathes steadily
in silence.

The baby in row 11 wails.
His ears hurt, thinks the mama.
She starts to shush and rock her child.
The papa points out the window
with a shaking hand. Look.
Now the mama rocks and prays,
singing the lullaby her mama sang to her:
Sleep, baby, sleep.
Sleep, baby, sleep.
She calls on all of the angels of God
to spare her only child.
If this impossible thing is happening
maybe a miracle is possible too.

The businessman in seat 3A gives up
doodling on his expense report
and cries for the child that
he won't see grow up; for the wife
he won't kiss again; for ever leaving home
for a stupid business trip. The businessman thanks God
for life insurance, hopes that his wife never finds
those pictures tucked up and zipped into
his briefcase pocket: Please, God,
spare her that. And mama,
meine gelibte mutter,
I love you.

The pilot backs up,
lunges at the unrelenting door.
The copilot breathes steadily
in silence.

The retired grandma in row 22
closes her eyes
thanks heaven for this last week
with the children
and their children, precious
kindele; she wings a prayer
to her best friend through all these
last long years; remembers
being fond of her husband,
and prepares to meet him
and her blessed mother
when the plane plunges
into the blanket of snow
spread over the rugged mountains.

The bass baritone in row 9,
whose honeyed low notes
resonated with dramatic emotion,
is reduced to sobbing and calling out
for Ave Maria,
Mother of God.

The pilot shouts orders and codes,
thrashing at the door.
The copilot breathes steadily
in silence.

The stewardesses hug each other.
They know crash position
won't do a damn thing.
They think of the hours spent
trying to identify the enemy in the crowd
while all along evil
was standing beside them,
in uniform. And this is how
it will end.

The high school boy in row 17
is sorry that insisting on sex
ever made Annika cry;
hopes his father remembers
how proud he was
when he made that basket at the buzzer,
and when he stood up to those
jerks at the park, even though
the kid they were picking on
really was a dork.

The pilot steadies himself
pictures his mother, young and
tender and sleepy, tucking him
back into bed. He apologizes for
his hubris. The pilot, bellowing,
tries to overthrow fate
but he can't.

The baby in row 33 puts her hands
to her ears and shrieks. Her mama
screams too, counting her rosaries
on baby's flexed toes,
begging forgiveness
for minor forgettable sins.

The copilot, breathing steadily
in silence, disables all alarms
overrides auto-corrections
and recalibrates
his deliberate descent.

The American mother and daughter in row 27
clutch hands as the earth hurtles closer;
the mother closes her eyes, refuses to believe;
the daughter screams "What is happening?"
over and over, as if
translating into a different language could
change the certain course.

The unthinkable happens:
  the plane crashes in flames.

For days the crews search at the Ravin de Rosé,
melted snow refrozen around
chunks of char and melted metal. They find
scattered teeth and bones. They report
headaches, some nausea, some
shortness of breath. Possibly
high altitude sickness; the plane
hit the mountain at 5,000 feet. Possibly
the sudden release of 150 souls
returned to stardust and ash.
At night the inspector from the local village
goes home, scrubs away the grit and
warms his hands; climbs into bed
giving thanks for his home and family,
for the mother who loved him and the father
who raised him to be the kind of man
who walks into the wreckage of hell and
tries to mend it, or at least
comprehend. He prays for a dreamless sleep,
but awakens again and again
to the phantom cries
of the anguished pilot
banging
on the cockpit door.

The reporter on the spot
once so jaded and cynical
always good for another round of drinks
sets aside his cell phone
ceasing to follow and retweet;
turns off the TV with captions
the radio with constant commentary,

and closing his tired eyes, thinks back
to the last time he told his mother
he loved her; the last time
he saluted his father, lost in
old stories of a forgotten, predictable
war. The reporter is haunted
by the madness of the copilot
breathing steadily, in silence,
for the 10 long minutes
he dove towards destruction.
The restless reporter
feels his lips moving in prayer
for the eternal salvation
of the pilot
blocked
by the locked cockpit door.

Grateful for Good Neighbors
for Tom and Marge Crosby

Thank you, kind sir. You saw
something not right—a child?
a doll?—tossed awkwardly in a
pile of leaves. But what's important

is this: you stopped. You went back.
Out of your way, late for work,
you listened to that little voice—
something is not right—and you found

a small girl. A toddler, naked and weary,
burned and bruised—tortured—alone—
in that pile of wet leaves. And you and your wife,
you gathered that child up, in your
arms, in your coat, and you brought that
baby home. Thank you. In a crazy mad world

we are told to look for the helpers. And you,
you and your wife, on that morning, by that act,
you saved a small girl, and also
a shred of my soul.

Off the Trail
> *Remembering Gerry Largay*

When you find my body
please call my daughter. Tell her
her mama will be with her
always. Steady as the sun.

When you find my body
look for my car. There's a
jacket in there, snacks,
a map. I must have gotten lost.

When you find my body
breathe. Look at what you see.
Listen to the human noise
in the space between heartbeats;

feel the atoms warmed by the sun
or cooled in its absence. Maybe
there are others with you. Maybe
it is solely you in the woods.

When you find my body
I will no longer be cold or hungry.
Please, call my daughter.
Then, save yourself.

Every Addict is Somebody's Child
> *"I made sure my daughter died with good credit and no police record. Imagine that."*
>
> Doug Griffin, *The Heroin Crisis: Special Report, Newburyport News 12/21/15*

i
Grandma's pills are gone
again, and my wife's bracelet
from our 15th anniversary, it's
missing, and the fifty dollars
stashed in my toolkit
isn't there. What the hell.
If anything is broken,
daddy will fix it. But
deep deep inside
there's a hole
in her soul.

I get so angry. I yell and threaten
and tell her I'm done—
I've gone as far as I can go—
but then look at her and know
I will love and protect my child
for the rest of my life. So
I convince the cop she's a good kid
who got sleepy after curfew;
I drag her butt out of bed to the therapist
and to meetings and the unemployment office
when she loses her job. Again.
When she tells me
the lights are going out, daddy,
first I freeze and then
I pay the electric. I tell her
she needs to be more responsible
but she crumbles, crying, she has
disappointed me—again—
and she feels so bad, so bad.
So I hold her and tell her I love her,

but even while I'm hugging her I know
she's going out to use again
to smother this fresh pain.
Because deep down inside
there's a hole
in her soul.

ii
I was down in my work room
making something, making a mess,
thinking about how we got here
and what is wrong with that kid
and how do I fix this, how do I fix her—
  is this a disease
    or is that an excuse—
when there was a knock on the door.
And even though I told her a hundred times
this was going to happen—told her
some day she would wake up dead—
until the man in uniform said they
couldn't revive her, I never came close
to imagining how much it hurts.
So bad. My baby is
gone. All of my life
up until that day—
gone. When she died,
everything stopped:
when she died,
something
dropped.
Deep down inside,
there's a hole
in my soul.

Unarmed Combat: A Report from the Front
dedicated to the Stanford rape survivor and all our Doe sisters

[Note: if Marines were attacked at the rate
that women in this country are battered and raped
we would surely be at war.]

I remember sharing with you
a poem that began: I remember sharing with you
but it was about another man. And I remember swapping stories
of the loves of the past: silly stories
some wistfully romantic
others still so raw sarcasm
couldn't bind the tattered pride. So we
passed the bottle back and forth
and built ourselves a friendship,
stronger than our differences but
lighter than our ties. And I rejoiced
that I had found another
caring testing teasing brother.

                        i remember the horror
                        i remember screaming pleading and i got
                        no response i saw your face
                        freeze into an empty everyman.
                        i saw you lose your humanity as
                        you stripped me and stole
                        mine. i remember the pain i
                        cried your name you did not
                        hear me. a robot programmed to destroy
                        raper. rapist. raping. raped.
                        what does that leave me.

I remember sharing meals. I remember
systems to divide the cooking and the washing
but the order evaporated
before the dishes dried. I recall with
longing endless debates as we

explored, defined and rationalized
our experiences and ideals and our
goals. I have the souvenirs
from the places that we dragged each other to;
places I might not have had the impulse
or the courage to go alone.
And you said it was o.k.
to wake you if the dreams got bad.

                    and you became the nightmare. i tell myself
                    it's over but your shadow is between me
                    and anyone i meet while i'm awake.
                    i meet people who shouldn't see
                    the badness inside the essence of
                    me you must have found, have
                    smelled. knowing what i was you decided
                    to act. as new folks become familiar i
                    retreat into my darkness i
                    won't lead them to my fortress,
                    to lure me to an ambush
                    only outsiders control. duck and cover is
                    my m.o. don't kick back! lest they should
                    find me. there is safety
                    in staying
                    alone.

I remember growing
apart, and feeling warm to know
I was nestled in the background of your life
like you were settled in
mine. I felt empowered, able
to loosen the ties and go off on my own,
returning not for reassurance but

with delight. I was gladdened to see
that I could be a friend,
that I had made an impact
in the structure of your self.

        i prowl through relationships now
        searching for clues to tie the
        spoken with the felt, the expression
        with the act because i know
        i was wrong once: i put
        my trust into a monster and i paid
        a heavy price. i don't know
        if the fault lay in the perception
        or in the thing to be perceived. i
        think of you now as a terrorist if
        i think of you at all, which happens
        less than it used to but
        more than i would like. i want to be cured
        but the scar can never heal
        and if it did i myself would rip it open.
        i know there is no threat that i can use
        no chip with which to barter for my safety.
        i imagine you walk through your world unscathed
        by the impotent hatred i carry
        for you. i fantasize ways
        to teach you what i have learned (there is no
        safe space) to expose you
        for the rotten walking corpse that you are
        and i arise no more rested
        than if i had slept
        and dreamed.

I remember waiting that whole long night
for the sun to arise and protect me. As
the hours dragged I turned on myself:
Sneering there could be nothing left to fear yet
too cowed to venture forth I cringed and stayed,
as if shelter alone could keep me
from harm. Etched into the darkness
was the outline of a cage
a trap disguised as a steadfast sturdy shield
and the locks and the bars
beckoned to me. I relived
every step we ever took, wondering where
I had erred. I blamed myself
then. I spent countless hours
alone in my silent
shame I have spent years
atoning for your
sin. And that
was the hardest battle
to win.

Because

Because I survived
I must speak out;
Because I survived
I must blend to pass.

Because I have endured
    months in your wards and
    hours crawling the floors of welfare offices,
    stared through plate glass windows of restaurants
    hungering in the streets,
    I have seen the naked bones
    of society's fortress.

Because I have emerged, risen from ashes
    earned degrees by day, working
    flat on my back through long groping nights,
    have learned to walk and talk and
    dress like you, to carry credit cards
    and expense receipts,
    I must blind myself to my past.

Because I have been scarred
I must be a revolutionary.

Because I have tasted your brand of success
I have learned to fear passion and loss.

What If

What if today
there were no shootings.
What if today, there were no
beatings, even if dinner is
late or cold. What if today
everyone had enough dinner.
What if today, those who call themselves
lovers actually respected each other.
What if today, children were
seen and believed and
treasured. What if today
we greeted our neighbors.
What if today
is all the time we have;
what if today
is enough;
what if.

Elizabeth S. Wolf writes because telling stories is how we make sense of our world, how we connect with our world, how we heal, and how we celebrate. Through years of interesting times, her catchphrase was "just another chapter for the book". Elizabeth lives in Massachusetts with her daughter and works as a metadata librarian.

Elizabeth has published poetry in anthologies (*Amherst Storybook Project; Mosaics: A Collection of Independent Women, Volume 1; The Best of Kindness: Origami Poems Project; Merrimac Mic Volumes I, II, & III*), and journals (*New Verse News, Scarlet Leaf Review, Peregrine Journal*). Her story "Lost and Found" is included in *UnCommon Minds: A Collection of AIs, Dreamwalkers, and other Psychic Mysteries*. Some of Elizabeth's earlier poetry in *The Valley Women's Voice* is included in the Valley Women's History Collaborative, a special collection of the UMass Amherst Libraries. Follow Elizabeth at amazon.com/author/esw

www.ingramcontent.com/pod-product-compliance
Lightning Source LLC
LaVergne TN
LVHW041505070426
835507LV00012B/1333